THE SELF-GUIDED GURU

LIFE LESSONS FOR
THE EVERYDAY HUMAN

VIOLETTE DE AYALA

The Self-Guided Guru, Life Lessons For The Everyday Human

ISBN-13: 978-0-578-57328-1 (ebook)
ISBN-13: 978-0-578-60469-5 (print)

Cover Design: inkberries.com
Illustrator: Alona Savchu
Interior Design: M. Okpako
Stay in touch with the author: www.violettedeayala.com

Dedicated and inspired by my spiritual advisors, Victoria, Angela, Nikki, Nora and my soulmate, Stephen. I am very grateful to my beautiful friend, Catalina who held my hand through this creative process.

CONTENTS

PROLOGUE

Each one of us holds the answers within ourselves to heal from the past, connect with our purpose and find joy in our path. The Self-Guided Guru takes you on a personal journey using 10 life lessons while asking engaging and profound questions that unleash the hold that blocks so many. Lessons include a personal mantra template, action steps and a recap to allow the reader to open the door to self-discovery. Each of us have different barriers, challenges and struggles that can not be addressed with a cure-for-all approach, however, we all have the power to be our own personal guru by answering the right questions and finding our own self-guided path.

HOW TO GET THE MOST OUT OF THE SELF-GUIDED GURU

1. Before reading a lesson, clear your mind for 5-10 minutes using silence or soft music. I recommend light meditation, prayer or simply closing your eyes before you begin a lesson.

2. Put away your phone and devices to avoid distractions before, during and after.

3. Each lesson is to be read one at a time allowing a minimum of 15 to 30 minutes for the self-guided worksheets.

4. Each chapter includes a mantra template to help you create your own personalized guru mantra.

5. Keep a pencil and paper handy to do your self-discovery and self-guided work. I love the idea of having a special journal dedicated to this book.

6. This work is about you and your journey. Be open to self- discovery and finding honest answers within your self- guided work. If you are not honest with yourself, the work will not be successful. There are no correct or incorrect answers.

7. When you have difficulty answering a question, write without thinking. Being stuck in your response means you have a block that needs to be worked through. Start writing and keep writing, soon you will find some clarity through your own words.

8. Work through the self-guided worksheet after each lesson as they were created to be done in unison with the lesson.

INTRODUCTION

Much of the world aches. At times, we think it's just us, but it's more common than not. No matter the history, there is some level of pain and unease in all of us. This level of pain or series of struggles holds humans back from moving forward in clarity, purpose, drive and sharing their light with others. When we selectively and intentionally stop ourselves from moving forward in our grandest strength, it impacts others around us and how their lives would benefit from our healing.

Most humans have a profound story related to how their limiting thoughts were created. Each of us has the intentional choice to either remove ourselves from the past and the pain that it holds or constantly reliving the defining moments that stifle our souls. It's a choice made robotically and without thought and it perpetuates into a life of more challenges and limitations or peace and opportunities.

What makes humans move forward and utilize their past to gain their deepest strength?

How are some of them able to look within and discover their purpose?

Why do some humans walk confidently into their greatness?

What makes us look within and embrace the need to evolve?

Each one of us makes life-changing decisions every day. If each moment has the power to shift our world, then every minute has the potential to be beautiful magic.

Every moment is a chance for us to shift up in our world and evolve. Every minute, we have the choice to live with yesterday's trauma or awaken anew. Yet so many of us dwell in the history of our past versus embracing the amazing opportunities and life-changing moments of today.

Picture a world full of humans living to their fullest potential, with the greatest fulfillment of their personal purpose achieved, while positively impacting, loving and assisting each soul they encounter along the way. Envision a global collective presence of evolved humans conducting life through the lens of love, self-love and clarity. The evolution of each of us works in part with others in our collaborative connection to love and be of service to one another.

I've journeyed down the road to becoming a better human. It was not pretty or in any way easy. I am not a perfect human, but I am better than I was last year and the year before. It's a conscious choice I make to strive for clarity, connectivity and improvement each day.

Through the narrative of my personal stories in the Self- Guided Guru, I intend to share the biggest life lessons I have learned and how they moved me to serve and connect to an authentic purpose and a profound love with an abundance of success. I hope that my lessons help you to discover the best version of you so you can shine brighter and change your world, and those of the ones around you to a greater state of purposeful living. The messier the self-discovery, the more profound the results.

Let's start.

Lesson 1:

HEALING

I wore metaphorical rose-coloured glasses for decades. They allowed me to see everything in the most beautiful and blinding light. It became comical that in the direst of situations, I always seemed to laugh and toss the seriousness out. Through self-discovery, I realized that I was using this mechanism to keep away the healing my soul needed and craved. I couldn't resist giggling when life seemed doomed. I was content with my way of subconsciously twisting the world to work in my favor so that it all looked pretty and perfect. This prevented me from acknowledging that my past hurt my evolution and kept me from the mandatory rebirth I needed to experience in order to move forward and heal.

Years went by and I found a growing restlessness in my heart. It felt like an introductory calling to be healed from childhood trauma. The laughter seemed to not be as prevalent and it was replaced with flashbacks of the not-so- good years. My internal damaged and suffering child crept into my mind and soul. I eventually transitioned into a state of peace through healing measures of self-discovery and honest reflection. While sharing my story, my healing coincided with the healing of others and my resolve became stronger. It was here that I was able to find purpose from my past. It's almost like it gave others a reason to also mend their past and move forward in their lives while giving me permission to do the same. The power of healing in collaboration with other humans is miraculous. The narrative of my childhood and the resulting limitations had, in various ways, been the sticking point of my personal growth,personal possibilities and my soulful evolution.

I grew up in an abusive home. My mother had episodes of good moments that I only recognized after processing the pain. I have a handful of fond memories and I hold onto those as part of the continual healing process. The hardest bump to get over was accepting that her lack of love and levels of abuse did not dictate the love I was able to receive or the beautiful love I deserved. Through her unkind stream of words, drug abuse and rollercoaster bouts of tainted love, I questioned what kind of love the world would hold for me if the one guaranteed love celebrated in every culture was non- existent for myself? If my mother didn't love me in a normal way, like the love all of the fictional and non-fictional mothers, then what kind of healthy love would be realistic for me to discover and accept? We accept the love we think we deserve.

My love story was riddled with highs and lows. Great abusers are very talented at making their victims' grandest purpose to love and adore them all the while instilling decades of pain through hostile words and actions. How can we take this emptiness and transform it into a life filled with love, acceptance, and unconditional peace?

I have finally been able to heal and experience blessings through phases of self-discovery and internal spiritual guidance. My mother passed away recently from her addiction and the sadness of the permanency of not having a loving biological mother was difficult. It indeed held me back and created destructive behaviour patterns. But I also found the brightest light within myself from these darkest moments. These storms make us stronger by choice.

Whatever you have endured, know that you have a larger strength within. What you think is your definition and your worth based on your painful past, is inaccurate and you can powerfully define your own worth and beauty. As you read this, give yourself permission to heal where needed. You deserve to live a life of full grace and deep peace. It is up to you to find your own closure and embrace the grand life waiting for you on the other side of your past because those storms have also strengthened your soul.

SELF-GUIDED WORKSHEET

My intention in sharing this worksheet is to ask the questions to the answers that hold your healing. These discoveries are crucial in your journey towards a bigger and brighter living.

Please note: I am not a therapist. I recommend seeing a licensed and trained therapist for professional therapy.

1. What childhood story or stories do you play over and over in your mind that hold you back? If your present life is not flourishing or you find that your life is at a longstanding pause, there is most likely a childhood self-limiting experience or interpretation that is holding you back.

_____

_____

_____

_____

_____

_____

_____

_____

_____

_____

_____

_____

2. What stories from your adult years are holding you back? Often, experiences from your adult years are connected to a life-changing experience from childhood which strengthens your inability to move forward in ways you envision and desire.

_____

_____

_____

_____

_____

_____

_____

_____

_____

_____

3. How is this defining you?

_____

_____

_____

_____

_____

_____

_____

_____

4. Re-write your childhood stories and make yourself your own hero now write it from that perspective.

_____

_____

_____

_____

_____

_____

_____

_____

_____

_____

5. Re-write the stories from your adult years and make yourself your own hero and write them from that perspective.

_____

_____

_____

_____

_____

_____

_____

_____

_____

_____

6. What action steps do you need to take to start to heal from your childhood?

_____
_____
_____
_____
_____
_____
_____
_____
_____

7. What action steps do you need to take to start to heal from your adult years?

_____
_____
_____
_____
_____
_____
_____
_____
_____
_____

8. What do you look forward to creating in your life once this does not hold you back?

_____

_____

_____

_____

_____

_____

_____

_____

_____

_____

_____

9. How will you feel when you can heal enough to move forward?

_____

_____

_____

_____

_____

_____

_____

_____

_____

_____

10. What will you say to yourself if you find yourself repeating the self-limiting words, talk or phrases?

_____

_____

_____

_____

_____

_____

_____

THE GURU SYNOPSIS

To move forward in your natural and unique greatness, healing is a necessary component. When we heal, we remove the layers of self-doubt and self-limiting thoughts. Humans able to heal, use the past as a way to not only stabilize their growth but to move forward out of the darkness. There is beauty in healing and saying, "The past does not define my highest potential and greatness".

PERSONAL MANTRA TEMPLATE

My past does not dictate my future.
What others may have done to me is not my story,
it's their story and it doesn't define me.
I am in complete control of my life
and the divine evolution
of who I am.
I allow myself to heal and
I allow myself to move forward in full grace.

What is clarity? Clarity is knowing in your soul your absolute purpose in life. Clarity means that you say no to situations and people that do not align with you, and you instinctively connect to those that feel right. Clarity is having a purpose that lights you up from within and it shows others that clarity is the inner guide we should all strive for.

To live with clarity is waking up in the morning, knowing what you will do with your day and life, using your intentional and purposeful guide to get you there, with a connection that is so strong that nothing distracts you from this hold on your vision.

Are people just born with clarity? Not really. It takes time to develop the power to find clearness in your mind in order to attract and move towards that which makes your spirit sing. The more time we spend attaining clarity, the easier it is to hold and make it an involuntary component of our lives.

Clarity also incorporates feelings, emotions and nonverbal confirmations. When I have strong connections to clarity, I feel a sense of grace around me. I also feel a sense of divinity and alertness. For some humans, it may be an aha moment that propels a guided move without realizing the steps. Some have these moments in a sequence guiding them to their larger purpose. The most significant moments of clarity can occur by starting with little strides that give way to consecutive steps that capture the larger purpose with gradual levels of confirmations.

What do I do with my life? What is my purpose? I can't seem to connect to my alignment. Why do I feel lost? Do these sound familiar?

Let's dive in and see where your clarity is waiting for you.

We all have unique gifts and talents given to us. Often, we have expanded on these natural-born talents through classes, experiences, studies and profound self-work.

Humans often get caught up in the chaos of the busy components in their surroundings. Between the likes, comments, shares, family, work and to-do lists, we start to feel at times a disconnect to our purpose, our alignment and our path. We lose our way to clarity through the robotic noise of the hustle, loudness and chaos.

While growing a business, balancing life and all the tasks in between, how do humans stay connected to what's really important? How do humans find and stay on the path towards clarity?

When I feel a bit upside down and lost in my constant state of motion, these are 12 exercises I use to get connected to my purpose and regain clarity. You may connect to your clarity and then need to reconnect to it as you up-level your life. That is a natural process and flow for your intentional evolution.

My intention with this guide is to help you find clarity and reconnect to it when needed.

SELF-GUIDED WORKSHEET

1. What is your superhero talent?

_____

_____

_____

_____

_____

_____

_____

_____

_____

2. What is the one talent you were given that makes you so incredibly special and gifted? Is it the way you can connect with humans in a rapid way? Is it finding solutions by thinking out of the box? Is it the way you can sense someone else's challenges? Is your talent listening to what another person is asking for? We all have an amazing and beautiful gift with its own unique flair. What is yours?

_____

_____

_____

_____

_____

3. How do you use your superhero talent to help others? Thinking of your #1 talent, how does that help others in their life and business? Does it help them find their perfect home? Does it help them find meditation through yoga practice? Does it help them manage their business better? We all have the power to make the lives of others better. How do you use your Powers for Good?

_____
_____
_____
_____
_____
_____
_____

4. How can you serve the world more profoundly? Now, if you have bridged the two biggest components in finding your purpose, how can you take this connection to your purpose and serve greater?

_____
_____
_____
_____
_____
_____
_____

5. How can you amplify your work to others in your family, community or around the world?

_____

_____

_____

_____

_____

_____

6. How can you share this talent to impact in a bigger way?

_____

_____

_____

_____

_____

_____

7. Your superhero talent has the purpose of helping others. What more can you do to serve to a brighter capacity?

_____

_____

_____

_____

8. What are habits, entanglements or behaviours that you must release in order to focus on your connection to clarity? (one to three is fine)

_____

_____

_____

_____

_____

_____

_____

_____

_____

_____

9. What are some activities that you can take on to bring forward a stronger connection to your clarity and your work?

_____

_____

_____

_____

_____

_____

_____

_____

_____

_____

10. How will you keep yourself accountable in the pursuit of your clarity, purpose and action?

_____

_____

_____

_____

_____

_____

11. What will you do to ensure that you keep moving forward with your new connection to clarity in your life?

_____

_____

_____

_____

_____

12. What will you do when you disconnect again and struggle to find the purpose?

_____

_____

_____

_____

_____

If you are hiding your talents because of fear, it's time to remove the shell of hinderance. If you are playing small with intention, you are intentionally not serving those around you to your greatest power. It's time to acknowledge your worth, value and the beauty you radiate and help others do the same. When we share our brightest light, it gives others permission and desire to do the same.

What will you do now to move forward towards your biggest and brightest light?

THE GURU SYNOPSIS

Humans connected in clarity do not compare themselves with the acts and ongoings of others. Their worth isn't tied to another person's perceived worth. They are content in their path because their connectivity to their alignment is concise and confirmed. Humans abundant in clarity do not waiver, they stick to the winding path and know in their soul it will all work out imperfectly perfect.

PERSONAL MANTRA TEMPLATE

I seek to live a life of clarity.
I desire to live a life of purpose.
I was born with beautiful
and unique talents that only I hold.
I am a blessing to those around me.

Lesson 3:

BALANCE

Some of the biggest topics humans like to discuss are mindset, balance, and clarity. Years ago, I was suffering from physical and medical ailments. I had been diagnosed with a torn ACL, 3 herniated discs, asthma, Hashimoto's, and pre-diabetes. I was a self-proclaimed and proud workaholic raising three children and active as a boardmember of six different non-profits and municipal organizations. I was PTA mom, volunteer extraordinaire and becoming very sick, in part due to all of my commitments. I was seemingly doing a great job and shining in all areas of my life which reinforced my behaviour and my continuous 'yes' to all proposed opportunities.

My blood pressure rose when I turned 39 and my body started to cry out. The kids were in 3 different schools and we had teams of babysitters to grab the pieces that were falling. I knew life had to change but I couldn't figure out how to get off of the insanity roller coaster. I was deeply connected to the concept that success meant being overwhelmed and never pausing. I truly believed that if I removed the chaos in my life, my worth would diminish, and the outward perception would depict me as a failure.

One afternoon, with my record high blood pressure, I was chatting with my physician in his office when he grabbed my phone and left the room, leaving me in the dark and disconnected. I sat alone for a few minutes, wondering how long he would leave me in his office without a connection to my wifi life. Fifteen minutes later he came back and handed me my phone. He took my blood pressure again and WOW! My blood pressure had returned to normal and his verbal prescription followed, "Slow down, smell the flowers and you'll be fine."

I tried to meditate and while in my solitude, my mind seemed to unravel with random thoughts at first. I started with short 30-second intervals and gradually worked my way up to 10 minutes just sitting in stillness and in peace. I started to take longer walks with the dog and left the headphones and my Sirius subscription at home. I then said 'no' to a few opportunities and this gave way to saying bigger 'nos'. Little by little, I regained my health by simply doing less.

I read up on balance and found little but a few articles and books that said balance was not a reality. I knew there was a formula waiting to be discovered on how to achieve balance and peace in life. I grew up in a charged home where violent scenarios were common. Using childhood as a guide wasn't an option. I spent time working on my balance and documented a process to share with other humans. Years ago, I finally achieved my inner balance and I still remain internally and externally successful in this achievement.

Here is my formula for achieving balance in your life. If you need a reminder of why balance is good, look at your health, wellbeing, and state of happiness. Could they be better? Are there pieces that need attention? Humans can always strive to better in these three areas.

My formula and your self-guided work

There are three components in each of our lives; happiness, health and wealth. We all have these three circles and they are all equally important because each activity, commitment, and responsibility falls within them. Here is how I define them.

HAPPINESS

This circle is about anything that makes your soul soar and your spirit connect with joy. This can be spending time with friends, a girls' night out, cuddling up with Netflix, a good book or walking the dog down a new undiscovered path. What brings you joy? What seems to increase your happiness level? Who are you with when you experience elevated levels of happiness? What are you doing? It'simportant to acknowledge your own personal definition of happiness.

HEALTH

This circle is all about your well-being. For me, this means taking the time to move my body and nourishing my physical vehicle with the finest food that supports optimum health. This also means taking time to meditate, a dip in the ocean, a walk in the park, yoga, or a much-needed spa retreat. Any action that elevates your health level and makes your human car run better and at its best, fits right here in this circle.

WEALTH

This circle is about your financial state. You don't have to be a millionaire or have 5 businesses to get this one in alignment. Wealth means a connection to money, control of expenses and savings. It means that wealth and the thought of money play an active role in your life through intention, thought and behaviour.

The concept of this balance formula is that each of the three circles must be consciously focused on with intention to always be in harmony with each other.

Struggling to find balance comes about when one of these circles is out of alignment.

Here are 3 examples of 3 humans not in balance:

- Barbara has a thriving yoga studio. She works around the clock, pays down her student loans and has started to save money. She is in great physical shape and teaches 20 classes a week. Her wealth and health circle are in check. However, she hasn't taken time off or done anything outside of work that brings her joy. She is feeling chaotic, tired and exhausted. Her balance is off. She must work on her happiness circle.

- Joan is a stay-at-home mom of three. She serves as PTA Chair and runs the school's annual fundraiser. She does Pilates 3 times a week and is training for a marathon. Her partner doesn't know about her credit card debt or spending habits. Her health and happiness circle are in unison. However, her wealth circle needs a drastic action plan.

- Lilly is a CPA and loves her girl-time. She and her friends have been close for decades and they dedicate a few days a week to social connectivity and giggle-time. They travel often and she makes a great salary. As a result, she just finished paying off her home mortgage. She is so busy that she just goes from the office to happy hour and the finest restaurants with no space between. Her wealth and happiness circle are complete and in balance, but her health needs attention.

SELF-GUIDED WORKSHEET

1. How is your happiness circle on a scale from 1-10? (10 being the absolute best)

_____

_____

2. How is your wealth circle on a scale from 1-10? (10 being the absolute best)

_____

_____

3. How is your health circle on a scale from 1-10? (10 being the absolute best)

_____

_____

4. Where does your attention need to be?

_____

_____

_____

_____

_____

_____

_____

5. What will you start to say 'no' to so you can find your balance?

_____
_____
_____
_____
_____
_____
_____
_____
_____
_____

6. What will you start to say 'yes' to so you can find your balance?

_____
_____
_____
_____
_____
_____
_____
_____
_____
_____

7. What other changes do you know have to happen?

_____

_____

_____

_____

_____

_____

_____

_____

_____

_____

_____

8. How dedicated are you to making these changes?

_____

_____

_____

_____

_____

_____

_____

_____

_____

_____

_____

9. How will you feel when you make these changes?

_____

_____

_____

_____

_____

_____

_____

_____

_____

_____

10. What will you do to make yourself accountable?

_____

_____

_____

_____

_____

_____

_____

_____

_____

_____

_____

THE GURU SYNOPSIS

The soul wants to feel in alignment in a well-rounded capacity. It thrives in harmony, peace and calmness. Often humans struggle with this because the disconnect from balance is so severe. When we were younger, we generally had balance naturally. Imagine waking up each day not rushed, pressured or in a frenzy. Envision having all aspects of life in a good state of flow. You may find yourself on various edges of balance during unexpected life changes, but working on this will help to make the necessary shift. Your soul craves tranquillity and the removal of stressful living.

PERSONAL MANTRA TEMPLATE

Achieving balance is possible.
My life is intentional and by my design.
I prioritize my well-being.
When I am in a state of balance, my world is brighter

Lesson 4:
OPPORTUNITY

There are hundreds, if not thousands, of books on manifesting, creating your dreams and designing your life. I read most and nothing really changed in my life as a result.

I would elevate my level of work output, dreamed big, and grew frustrated on my journey to manifesting a great life.

It took a few years to figure it out. My intention for this chapter is to give you the secrets I learned when it comes to opportunity and manifestation.

Here is how manifesting really works

ENERGY

If you're constantly thinking you won't find love, money is always tight and people are out to get you, you will attract all of that negativity into your life. You may live random moments in a high state of energy waiting for the manifestation to start, but life won't evolve if you revert to thinking the world is stacked up against you. You need to work on your energy and work to maintain a positive state of an elevated mindset for a significant period of time. When we doubt, worry, and think negative thoughts, an invisible cloud hovers over our heads and blocks the future arrival of happiness. You must work on maintaining that high and evolved level long enough to allow the opportunities to come through, so it reinforces the reality that you have the power to create and design your life. Once we see one beautiful nugget of flourishing opportunity come into our lives, we can propel ourselves to stay connected to continuous positive thinking. Often humans revert to negative thinking after a hiccup or bump in the road and it creates a cyclical pattern of frustration and depletes our goal orientated strengths.

ACTION

I see a lot of humans thinking happy thoughts, elevating their thinking and then, an opportunity shows up and they don't grab it. Opportunity comes to you through another human and it's most likely clothed as something small and perhaps insignificant. Small glimpses into a window of opportunity once taken, leads us to greater opportunities. Millions of dollars will not show up at your door because you meditated on stacks of green paper. It shows up because perhaps you met someone at an event, and followed up, showed action and accountability and then it led to layers upon layers of opportunities. You must take quick action when an opportunity that is in synch with your clarity presents itself. There is no sustainable get rich scheme. You must work for it and show up at the highest level of integrity. As my friend Nora says, "You've got to show up and do the work."

ACCOUNTABILITY

When the opportunity shows up and you grab it, be accountable! That means do the work beyond expectations, give more than is expected, be a person of your word. The world is filled with humans that take on commitments, promise the moon and stars and then don't communicate, stop short of doing the work and/or blame others. Don't be a blamer. Show integrity in all you touch. Those around you are watching and as you do something with purpose, you do everything.

PERSISTENCE

A majority of humans give up before they hit the goal. Then they wonder why life isn't lining up for them. Some people do one spurt of work and expect to be named CEO moments later. Be persistent in your work and for the long term. No one cares if you did one thing correct out of 100. What matters is that you show up steadily and stay focused.

INTENTION

Humans can read your intention without a word spoken. If your intention is to make as much money as possible, regardless of the damage it may do to others, you need to be a better human. Your intention is perfected when it's in alignment with your superhero talent and the service you give to the world. What's your intention through the work you do and the life you want to lead?

The following is a story that shares the power of hidden opportunities and shows how each step aligned to manifest a bigger vision.

MEET INNA

I love meeting people while I travel. Inna is an amazing human being who has connected completely with the ability to attract opportunities and design her life based on her actions, all in alignment with her superhero talent and the life she envisions for herself. She manifested opportunity and when it came her way and she took action. I met Inna while in Portland, Oregon with FemCity work. She was my driver from the airport to the hotel.

After high school, Inna moved from Siberia to California with the intention of learning English. She had little money (a budget of $5 per day). Within a few months, she learned how to speak and write English. She then attended a local college while teaching piano and tutoring Russian. Years later, she graduated with a degree in hospitality and was later hired by a boutique hotel. She worked so hard and diligently that the hotel sponsored her path to citizenship.

She moved her way up through the hotel and married a fellow manager. They both took on two jobs and each worked 80 hours a week. Soon thereafter, Inna became pregnant and they realized they could not bring a child into the world while both were working 80 hours a week yet barely making ends meet.

She had a business idea. With negative $300 in their account, she figured out a way to rent a Lincoln Town car. Her husband became the driver and in one day they made $500. They continued this path and saved enough money to purchase their own Town Car. They were able to make more money and save more which then led to purchasing another car. Soon after, they added a Mercedes Benz van and a limo and they grew their business to handle the biggest corporate accounts in Portland.

She also realized that she loved the idea of being an aesthetician. She went back to school and got that license, too. She now owns a small boutique spa in the Pearl District and still runs her professional chauffeuring service.

HERE'S WHAT INNA CAN TEACH US.

1. She could have settled for life in Siberia, which she admitted would have been challenging. This shows us that we can indeed create the life we want.

2. She could have worked in a mediocre capacity at the first hotel and not have had the company sponsor her as a result. Show up and do great work when opportunity presents itself.

3. She had an idea and was able to make it happen. Even without money, she found a way. If we believe that we are meant to do more in our lives, we create opportunities with no excuses.

4. She wanted to start another company and found a way to organize her hours and design her life to give her options

while raising two beautiful girls. She didn't find excuses or blame others, she owned her situation and was accountable to her dreams.

5. She could have decided not to leave Siberia. She could have given up learning another language. She could have stayed the course working two jobs. She could have given up with each moment that was filled with struggle. Her mindset was set on not giving up!

SELF-GUIDED WORKSHEET

1. Where can you be more accountable?

_____

_____

_____

_____

_____

_____

_____

_____

2. What will you do to work on your energy? Hang out with happy people, read positive things, not watch TV or movies with negative narratives, etc.

_____

_____

_____

_____

_____

_____

_____

_____

_____

3. What areas in your life will you be more persistent in?

_____

_____

_____

_____

_____

4. What is your intention?

_____

_____

_____

_____

_____

_____

_____

5. How do you help others?

_____

_____

_____

_____

_____

_____

_____

6. What do you want to truly manifest?

_____

_____

_____

_____

_____

_____

7. What kinds of opportunities may lead you to your dreams?

_____

_____

_____

_____

_____

_____

_____

8. How committed are you to seeking and following through with opportunity? (On a scale from 1-10, 10 being all-in!)

_____

_____

_____

_____

_____

THE GURU SYNOPSIS

Humans hold themselves back when they blame others for their current state. Those who have looked within to work on themselves, accept responsibility and from there, move forward. They are in control of their lives and are graced with more opportunities. Humans who find opportunity, blessings and abundance all around understand that the world is working in their favor, and that it's up to them to show up and do the work. That, in turn, creates more opportunity and therefore, greater favor in the universe.

PERSONAL MANTRA TEMPLATE

I will seek opportunities.
When an opportunity arrives,
I will take action in full integrity and commitment.
I am a person of my word.
I understand to create the life I want,
I must do uncomfortable work.

Lesson 5:

WEALTH

I s wealth really a part of being a more evolved human? The majority of people struggle with their connection to finances. Often, it's because they have never properly learned about budgeting and spending in a logical, healthy manner. Society is constantly sharing imagery of luxurious lifestyles and the must-haves that go along with them. The on-going images of living beyond means create a patterned downfall for those trying to make ends meet. The constant brainwashing via advertisements and influencer postings depicting lives of excess deflate many humans in their aspirations and mandatory sustenance. {How about what's in red for: the aspirations of many and their everyday efforts to stay above water financially} This continues to create a disconnect with money and for a lot of people, a detachment to wealth and a wealth mindset.

When we disconnect from money, it's because we are overwhelmed with our current financial state and that takes energy away from being a better and more evolved human. When we find peace in our finances and connect to wealth in a positive and embracing way, we can then connect more profoundly to bigger acts of kindness and living in harmony within our daily existence. Many can't seem to catch up and struggle to find the finances to pay for their basic living expenses. This damages the soul and hinders our power because the anxiety of achieving this exaggerated lifestyle distorts our connection to the greatness we have yet to unleash.

Our wealth vibe is a critical part of being a better, happier and more solid human. There are two mindsets when it comes to how we connect to the world and money, the poverty mindset and a wealth mindset.

This is how I define them.

THE POVERTY MINDSET

This human looks at the world from the point of view of 'lacking', with a short-term vision of the future and is frequently in crisis mode. Their energy is frenetic and their vibe is one of desperation, unease and instability.

Words used by those suffering from the poverty mindset:

I can't, I won't, she has, they have, I wish, I'll never, I blame.

Thoughts by those with poverty mindset:

Things won't get better, my life is always a fight and struggle, everyone has help and I don't, they have everything it takes and I won't ever, the world is out to get me, I can't ever seem to catch up,

THE WEALTH MINDSET

This human looks at the world from the point of view of abundance, blessings, gifts all around them and there is a long term vision. They are in a state of flow and know that the world is always in alignment with their dreams. Their souls are easy, harmonious and calm with their energy.

Words used by those embracing a wealth mindset:

I can, I will, I love that she has, I always, I create, I do.

Thoughts by those with a wealth mindset:

I know things will get better, my life is always filled with opportunities and blessings, the world is in connection to assist me, I have everything it takes, I am responsible for the creation of my life.

Are we all born with a wealth mindset? Generally, yes. But through childhood and adult experiences and the way we connect to those stories and moments, the wealth mindset disappears, and it is then replaced by one of poverty. We can all make the shift into a wealth mindset. I often prescribe the money guide to those humans looking to make the shift.

THE MONEY GUIDE

I love sharing my Money Guide exercise. It's the first step into changing your mindset from poverty to wealth. Your wealth mindset is an invisible and metaphorical muscle that needs to be expanded and strengthened through exercises and experiences. The stronger this fictitious muscle gets, the more you pull your way out of the doom of bad money thoughts and into one of the grand wealth mindset.

INSTRUCTIONS FOR YOUR MONEY GUIDE

1. Get a journal specific to this activity. It's going to be your Money Guide. If you have a few dollars to spend, pick one out with intention. What looks like a Money Guide to you? Does it have hints of gold, fragments of green? If you don't have a few dollars to spare, I gotcha. Find a used notebook in your home or take a few pieces of paper and staple them together so you don't lose a page. If you are using arepurposed notebook, tear out the used pages and it will be refreshed and ready for your new mindset.

2. For the next 30 days, write down in your new Money Guide, all of the times that you come across a penny, a dime or even a dollar. Whether the penny is on the floor, below a sofa cushion, or falls out of your pocket while doing the laundry, jot it down!!!

Besides noting the tangible aspect of wealth, write down anytime you receive a gift. A gift can be a cup of coffee with a friend, a potted plant from a neighbor, a chocolate bar given by a colleague. It can also be when someone invites you to a networking event, sends you a code to get an item at a discount or a complimentary gift. This exercise will awaken your wealth mindset to see you have little tiny wealth blessings all around. The more you acknowledge them mentally and physically in your Money Guide, the more you will see and take notice of your current wealth blessings.

3. For the same 30 days and in the same Money Guide, you will also write down all of the new people you meet and the grandest possibility that relationship can bring to you, your brand and your wealth. If you are at a networking event and you meet someone that works as a social media marketer, perhaps knowing them will give you the tips you need to expand your business tenfold. For example, I was at a child's birthday party many years ago and befriended another mother there. Through our conversations, I could tell she was brilliant at business. She turned out to be one of my biggest mentors and now I see she has brought me over $100,000 worth of knowledge just from our mom talks.

Each person you meet is a gift who presents knowledge, inspiration, referrals and opportunities. Do you want to increase your wealth to pay for bills? Would you like to increase your wealth? This is the thinking you will need to get there.

SELF-GUIDED WORKSHEET

1. What poverty mindset words, phrases or action are you sharing internally that you will change today?

_____

_____

_____

_____

_____

_____

_____

_____

_____

_____

2. Write 1 sentence about your money story, in other words, when you think of money you think of...

_____

_____

_____

_____

_____

_____

_____

_____

3. Write 3 common thoughts you have about money.

_____

_____

_____

_____

_____

_____

_____

_____

_____

_____

4. Rewrite these 3 common thoughts about money using a wealth mindset.

_____

_____

_____

_____

_____

_____

_____

_____

_____

_____

5. What action steps do you need to take to move forward in your new wealth mindset?

_____

_____

_____

_____

_____

_____

_____

_____

_____

_____

6. What issues do you need to address to make this happen?

_____

_____

_____

_____

_____

_____

_____

_____

_____

_____

_____

7. How committed are you to your new wealth mindset work?

_____

_____

_____

_____

_____

_____

_____

_____

_____

_____

8. How will you hold yourself accountable?

_____

_____

_____

_____

_____

_____

_____

_____

_____

_____

9. How will you feel once you have a wealth mindset?

_____

_____

_____

_____

_____

_____

_____

_____

_____

_____

_____

10. Write your new money story.

_____

_____

_____

_____

_____

_____

_____

_____

_____

_____

_____

_____

THE GURU SYNOPSIS

Embrace the concept of wealth as a gift and blessing, not because of the dollar value, but because positive relationships include the giving and receiving of energy with an equal exchange of value. Recreate your money story, and shift into seeing the wealth already around you at this very moment.

KEEP IN MIND

Wealthy mindset people know their numbers.

- How much do you owe?
- How much do you spend?
- How much do you save?
- How can you cut down your expenses?
- How can you increase your money?

Wealthy mindset people seek to amplify their money.

- How can you grow your business more?
- How can you use your money to make more money?
- What long term vision do you have now with your new wealth mindset?

Wealthy mindset people hang out with other wealth mindset people. You have heard it before I am sure, "like attracts like".

- Who are the people around you who have a wealth mindset?
- Who has a poverty mindset?

I encourage you to surround yourself with those with a wealth mindset. I also encourage you to take this activity and do it with a friend so you can both level up together. Caring is sharing... as you know.

PERSONAL MANTRA TEMPLATE

I am worthy of abundance.
My money story makes me smile and I embrace wealth.
I will think of money in a long-term capacity.
My past mistakes with money
do not define my future wealth.

Lesson 6:

HEALTH

I was a sick little girl. I was born with asthma, a heart murmur and was unhealthy due to an overconsumption of Cuban food. I struggled with my weight since I can remember. Diet was an everyday word and became a part of me from the time I was 8-years-old. In middle school, I was obsessed with fitness and weight loss and it was then that years with my eating disorder began. I could spend days without eating while running a few miles after step aerobics and hours at the gym. It wasn't until I was 7 months pregnant with our first child that the doctor threatened me to eat or the baby would suffer. I then gained 60 pounds in 2 months and forever my stretch marks will remind me to keep my health in balance. The baby was born perfectly healthy and my journey to find a true way to optimum health started.

I purchased a subscription to Self and Shape magazines. I enlisted in a shake program that removed all carbs except for one little muffin, with permission to consume 3 oz of protein and tons of greens on a daily routine. I lost the weight in 2- pound increments and the launch of my first business was inspired as a result.

I started my first company at 22 as a certified personal trainer. I had no funds to get started, but I had a beautiful new Discover card. I got into the niche of helping other humans to lose weight and find their balance as well. Years later, I launched a Pilates studio and grew the studio to various satellite locations. I ran that business for about 10 years and loved every moment of my work. I witnessed physiques change and spirits lift as they found their new healthy bodies. Not all my students were a size 0, as each of our physical bodies has its own beautiful design and shape not dictated by measurement. Each student found a way to be their healthiest version and that was a blessing to witness.

Is being an evolved human all about being skinny? Absolutely not. But there should be a very strong connection to your physical and earthly vehicle and wanting it to perform at its designed best.

After training for nearly 15 years, having 3 children and going through a torn ACL, 3 herniated discs, pre-diabetes, Hashimotos, and becoming certified as a personal trainer and Pilates instructor, I will give you the 12 tips I wish all books would share.

IT'S PERSONAL

Your body performance and physique are unique and perfect by design. Whether you were born with a few differences or challenges, you are designed perfectly. The goal should be to create a healthy lifestyle that works for you. Not your neighbor, or bestie, but you. Don't attempt to be a size 0 or 6 ft. tall. Work on being your best healthiest state.

YOUR BODY IS DIVINE

When we go to church, or a wedding or a special gathering, we wear our best outfit and do our hair. Why? Because when it's a special occasion, we try to look our best. Now, take that same concept and repeat this mindset with your physical body. Nourish it with the best you have. Instead of investing in the latest fashion, invest in the supreme entity of you. Be selective with what you put in your body and what you put on your body. Choose the best quality of food you can afford. I was vegan for years and also on a budget of $150 a week for a family of 5. We did it! It's about being intentional with the items you pick and having them give you the most nutrition. Connect with the concept that food is medicine and healing.

LISTEN TO YOUR BODY

Whether it's Weight Watchers, Keto, Atkins, Vegan, Vegetarian, Pescatarian, Plant Paradox, there is likely an option that fits you. How will you know? You will feel better, your gut will stop having issues and your energy will increase. Try one plan that you feel is a good fit for 4-6 weeks. Write down how you feel, your energy and your gut feedback throughout your time on the diet. Your body will tell you what it wants and doesn't want. If you are constantly sick with cases of the flu or colds, if your stomach is uneasy, and your energy is low, look at your diet. What does your body seem to like and dislike and then edit and go forward. I have friends who did Keto and then had more success on Plant Paradox. I have friends who hated Atkins but loved and found results with Weight Watchers. Each body is different but it's always sending you messages of what makes it thrive and what is slowly making it unravel.

MOVE YOUR BODY

You don't have to do a triathlon. You don't need to be a yoga instructor. You can just move your body as much as you can throughout the day. Walk, stroll, run, spin, Zumba... pick the one you love to do! So often I see humans forcing themselves to become runners. If you don't like to run, don't do it. There are activities you can sign up for that will move your body. I love spinning 3 times a week, barre and weights 2-3 times a week and I toss in a few boot camps to get my body more adaptable. I find my body loves a good mix. What does yours like?

EXTERIOR BODY

Did you know that my favorite cream is coconut oil?! It's inexpensive and makes my skin glow. Be very conscious and intentional even with what you put on your skin and hair. Again, don't go crazy spending dollars on the latest Allure awards. Read the contents of what you are putting on your body and be smart about the ingredients. What you put on, goes in.

PRINCIPLES OF FOOD

What's a general rule for food? Green veggies as raw as they can go, lean proteins and healthy fats throughout the day. Limit or remove sugar, starches and beverages with calories.

MENTAL HELPS PHYSICAL

Practice moments of solitude, meditation, and/or prayer. Your mental state is connected to your health. Ten minutes a day just breathing with no devices or tech near you is one of the best things you can do for your brain.

SLEEP

A no-brainer! Sleep 7-8 hours a day. Easier said than done? Avoid caffeine, limit screen usage at night including cell phones and TV, transition your mind into a quiet space by whatever means work for you and ease into that 7-8 hour block of sleep. We all respond to different sleep stimulants, for some, certain teas work miracles, for others, it's daily exercise that does the trick. However, if you've tried it all and still find it hard to fall and stay asleep, it may be time to speak with your physician.

ADD HUMOR

I am happier when I watch happy things. Surround yourself with happiness, happy people, books, movies, sitcoms, etc. The world has enough negativity in it. You do not need to add more to your psyche.

LOVE YOURSELF

No matter what, be your healthiest state with the words you use and the way that you love yourself. When I was little, I so wanted to have white skin, blonde hair and blue eyes. I had to fall in love with the divine presence of my Cuban skin. You are imperfectly perfect. Be sure to fall in love with all of the blessings that make you, you!

SELF-GUIDED WORKSHEET

For this lesson, write a few paragraphs on what changes you will make, your commitment level, what you will do in order to make these changes consistent, and what actions you will take if you lose your way in creating a healthier you. When you have finished writing your new healthier way of living, sign, date and review this contract daily for at least 6 weeks.

THE GURU SYNOPSIS

The human body was designed to be honored, maintained and treasured. How we treat ourselves and our physical bodies show respect and kindness for our path and purpose. It is all connected. Honoring the way we rest, nourish, and move our bodies shares love with our soul. It is always a great thing to be respectful of our creation and physical being.

PERSONAL MANTRA TEMPLATE

I will honor my body by moving it daily.
I will respect my body by choosing nourishment that is best for maintenance.
I will intentionally rest, recharge and meditate.
My body is divine.

Lesson 7:
SELF-LOVE

Most humans misinterpret the word combo "self- love". When I first heard the term, self-love, I thought it was founded on narcissistic behaviour and based on those wanting to give excuses for their lack of drive and laziness. I had to discover what the trendy term meant so I did- by hitting rock bottom in an overly committed, stressful world all while aspiring to be Wonder Woman to all things and all people.

It wasn't until my soul felt so depleted that I started to crave intentional healing and mega doses of prescribed love of self. I was putting everything and everyone first in my strong desire to prove to the world that I could do it all, effortlessly. I don't know when the initial anti-self-love thoughts began to take hold, but it felt like from one day to the next, I was drowning in my own negative decisions and intentionally not caring about my well-being.

Thankfully, I woke up to the realization, as many of us do, that I was simply exhausted by life. The much needed and mandatory shift to embracing self-love was inspired by a decline and brokenness within me. Things were unravelling at work and at home. I couldn't find the time to rest and recharge. I was also very sick with quarterly bouts of pneumonia, sinus infections and intense colds. My body was telling me, "Ya need to slow down and give yourself some love".

During this time, I read about self-love. But like all things, messages don't resonate until you are suffering or craving the knowledge and resolve that benefit you at that moment. This is where I dove in, researched more and found the definition.

Self-love means that when the chips are down, I can reconnect with my soul and know that there are grace and beauty around. Self-love means that when ugly words are spoken to me, my soul continues to shine because I am solid in who I am. Self-loves means I rest, I meditate, and I take the time to charge my spirit because I am best when filled with healing energy. It means that the words I speak to myself are always uplifting, positive and abundantly supportive.

When we speak kindly to ourselves, we share kindness with our core. When we only build up and not tear down, we strengthen the foundation of our purpose and our alignment. When filled with self-love, we don't need superficial cheering up. Love and radiance come from within and it roars with strength when self-love is embraced. When you are filled with self-love, you are prepared to create the life you deserve, and you no longer make excuses. When you find yourself between the different levels of no self-love or poor self-love, the excuses you share internally keep you in the world of mediocrity. Excuses often come from a lack of loving oneself.

Self-love, as I define it, is to listen to your physical body and mental state, share praise, kind words and schedule moments of healing and recharge. Just as we do with our phones, iPads, laptops and cars, the human body and mind also need moments of rest and rejuvenation.

These steps are how I embraced and infused more self-love in my life.

1. Your words: The words you allow to own space in your mind dictate the state of your own self-love. Ideally, the words you share internally should be words that bring out your best, strengthen your purpose and cuddle the uniqueness of your soul. When we think words that bring down our energy, reduce our power, diminish, or doubt our beauty, they remove the possibility to love ourselves. As you catch yourself thinking those not-so-kind words, replace them with words that derive from a place of love. Rewire your brain to be your best friend, your biggest champion and the cheerleader of your profound greatness.

2. Words to others: When chatting it up with friends, family or loved ones, are the words coming from a place of love?

As we speak to ourselves, we speak to others and our view of the world is encapsulated by the combination. When others aren't around, are you still sharing kind words? If you say harsh words to others, it may be rooted in your own lack of self-love. Catch yourself when your words come from a place of non-love and redirect the conversation to form a beautiful image of others. How we see the world, is how we see ourselves.

3. Moments that bring you joy: We generally connect self-love with spending dollars at the spa or on an item that serves as a reminder of pseudo-self-love. I am a fan of spas and their purpose in my life is to bring joy in the stillness. I find self-love in moments of peace. Self-love isn't necessarily the items we buy, the paid experiences we take on, but the way it embraces our purpose and gratitude. Surround yourself with moments that lift your soul. Take a walk in the park, stroll on the beach, sit at a cafe to catch the sunset. What are the moments that bring you the most joy? Design your life around these moments and your self-love will soar. To see the beauty in the world, we must see the beauty within ourselves.

SELF-GUIDED WORKSHEET

1. What series of words do you commonly tell yourself that don't act to lift you?

_____

_____

_____

2. When was the last time you were really upset with yourself?

_____

_____

_____

3. What words did you use at the time?

_____

_____

_____

4. What are 5 words that come to mind about who you are?

_____

_____

_____

5. What do you tell yourself when things go wrong?

_____

_____

_____

6. When was the last time you were proud of yourself for something you took on?

_____

_____

_____

7. When was the last time you got yourself out of a funk with your own kind words?

_____

_____

_____

8. What are 5 beautiful words that describe your greatest talents and gifts?

_____

_____

_____

9. What are ways you praise yourself when you accomplished a task?

_____

_____

_____

10. What do you tell yourself when things go right?

_____

_____

_____

THE GURU SYNOPSIS

You must remove thoughts, words and behaviours that are holding you down, exhausting you and blocking your higher level of self- love to flourish. Whether they are ways of thinking, things you say, activities or people, the goal is to remove as much as you can and add words and behaviours that lift your soul, activities that make you smile and people who make your spirit grow with joy and grace. Be intentional, conscious and aware of the need to increase your self-love.

PERSONAL MANTRA TEMPLATE

I am enough and imperfectly perfect.
I am my biggest fan and cheerleader.
I will only share kind thoughts and words when internally speaking.
I will only share kind thoughts and words when externally speaking.

Lesson 8:

LOVE

There are two ways to look at the world: through loving eyes or through un-loving eyes. The choice is there for us all. Humans who see the world through loving eyes shine more and their energy is more contagious. These love-filled humans walk into a room and the room brightens up. They are infectious and know they radiate kindness and love.

Thinking of the most loving people you know in your life, I am sure just the thought of them makes your heart smile.

Often these humans didn't always have love in their world. But they evolved enough to recognize that it is much better to live life through love than the alternative. Humans who view the world through love, know that life will always work out, that the world will be fundamentally blessed for them and even though they also have pain and suffering, they find the beauty in the darkest of moments because of their soulful evolution.

Humans who look at the world through a lack of love, look at the world with rage, bitterness and anger. The world has not been in their favor according to their interpretation. They generally use anger-infused words, share negative phrases and their connectivity to other humans is mostly strafed by conflict. These humans are uneasy, and they can also change the aura of a room with a cloud of static and chaotic energy. Thinking of the most non-loving people you know in your life, I am sure just the thought of them makes your heart uncomfortable and sad.

Why do some humans radiate love and some radiate negativity? It's a choice that each of us has at any moment. However, to look at the world through love, your soul must be connected to a greater purpose or something bigger than yourself.

Steve and I married at the young age of 22 and 24. We had an instant love-at-first site connection and managed a long- distance relationship until we tied the knot. Within 10 years, we had two children, remodeled a few historic homes, and had a fast-paced life filled with running businesses, raising babies and sustaining a healthy relationship with one another.

However, at our 20-year mark, having been through the highs and lows of life together through good moments and challenging ones, we divorced. We still loved each other but recognized that our relationship was no longer healthy and an intentional and purposeful disconnect was needed. We maintained a common household since we each travelled extensively for work. The set up was ideal for the circumstances as well as for the benefit of our children. We were respectful, loving and remained friends.

Years later, we found our way to each other again, this time more mature, further along in our healing, and happy in each other's arms. We had privately discussed giving it a go again as two independent and healthy humans with more clarity and stability within ourselves. After a few months of dating, we realized that the second time around had a more solid foundation, sustenance and a deeper soulful connection and existence. We share our story often to inspire others to form healthy, balanced and loving connections with other people who have evolved as well. We both had to step away, reflect and evolve in order to be better humans to ourselves and to one another.

These are 3 ways you can change your world view and step into one of more love:

It feels so good to see love no matter what you were born with or your past challenges and struggles.

1. The love starts with you: To see the world with an abundance of love and soulful radiance, you must love yourself, your past, and your current situation. Often humans are angry because things weren't what they thought they should have been when they were

younger, or someone did them wrong, or they made mistakes, bad choices or feel stuck. Whatever the reasons, when we shift from the place of lack of love for ourselves into a fully accepting love of all of our components, the shift into love starts to move. Each time you share unkind words, you bring down and diminish your light. The moments you say something ugly about yourself or others, you are keeping your spirit from moving forward into angelic love. The shift must start with you. To be a person of love, you must radiate love from your soul and that starts with just changing the way you think and speak about yourself and others. When people love their messy existence no matter what, they have truly started to love everything around them.

2. The love continues with others: As you start to see yourself in this imperfect light of love, you will start to see those around you in the same light. Share kind words with those around you and note the moments of gratitude with them. Others will note your shift and they will either embrace your love or rebuff it. Sometimes another human's light is so bright that it makes others very uncomfortable to be near. Remove gossip, ill tales and unkind thoughts of others from your life. A human of love doesn't share negative words.

3. Acts of love: Humans love acts of love. To shift into a heart of complete love, do activities that share kindness. This can be volunteering at a local shelter, adopting a rescue pet, doing a good deed. The more of these you do with no expectation of return, you will shift into a world of more profound love.

SELF-GUIDED WORKSHEET

1. What words have you been sharing that haven't been kind?

_____

_____

_____

_____

2. What new words will you add in their place?

_____

_____

_____

_____

3. What are a few social media posts you have made that perhaps didn't come from love?

_____

_____

_____

_____

4. What are the words, phrases, conversations you had that didn't come from love that you will now edit to change that?

_____

_____

5. How will you share more acts of love?

_____

_____

_____

_____

6. What activities will you take on to keep connected to love?

_____

_____

_____

_____

7. What action will you take on when you are feeling a disconnect from love?

_____

_____

_____

_____

8. How can you inspire others to share more love and kindness?

_____

_____

_____

_____

THE GURU SYNOPSIS

Life doesn't go right for every person based on what their expectations are. Most humans have had setbacks based on their own personal experiences and interpretation. Life is sometimes filled with difficulties and we all have challenges and struggles. Many don't share them on social media or with others. Be the human that chooses to love the world regardless of what society says should anger you. Choose to be the light in this world. And then empower others to also share their love and light.

PERSONAL MANTRA TEMPLATE

I accept the love I deserve.
I deserve healthy and uplifting love.
I will share only loving thoughts with other humans.
Without words spoken, I will radiate love with just my presence.

Lesson 9:
RELATIONSHIPS

It took me decades to develop healthy relationships. I finally recognized that relationships must be in a constant balance of giving and taking. I spent so much time being the giver and then feeling hurt or disappointed with the way others treated me in return. I felt constant conflict with the ebb and flow of most relationships in my life.

Every single relationship in life must be in balance, where both parties feel equally a part of it. Most humans experience being left out of invitations for gatherings or meet-ups. Some don't receive returned calls or texts with extended outreach. Being ignored can be one of the biggest heartbreaks.

One day, I shifted into a state of reality and finally understood the secret to relationships. Turns out, I was doing it all wrong.

Humans make time and give energy to those relationships they prioritize based on their own needs and wants. Those I was trying to be friends with didn't prioritize our relationship. As much as that concept hurt, it was true and it was not personal. We do not need to flow with all humans and sometimes we grow apart due to current priorities, personal development and the natural evolution of what serves us best. It was better for me to realize that this was not a bad thing nor did it reflect on me and my worth. It simply wasn't going to flow in a healthy way. And that's alright and it's still a gift.

Healthy relationships must find that sweet spot where give and take are in balance.

Here are three guiding principles to establish and maintain healthy relationships:

1. Communication: The conversations between humans that epitomize healthy relationships are fundamentally constructed on honesty, truthfulness and a loving connectivity. The words shared may be uncomfortably honest, but they are given from

a place of love. Verbal connectivity is balanced by love given and love receivedwith the words that are mutually shared. The same reflection occurs in the mimicked acts of kindness and respect. A confirmation that you're in a healthy relationship may be that your heart smiles almost always and your soul feels inflated with gratitude while chatting with this other human. You always feel better after connecting. That's a great sign that this relationship, friendship or partnership is a keeper.

2. Outreach: There is reciprocity in the exchange of invites and gatherings. The flow between the reach out is fairly balanced. Both parties in this scenario value one another's efforts and appreciate the coordination of connectivity. They equally want to spend time with one another, and the reciprocity is apparent and felt.

3. Value energetically: Each human in this scenario receives the same benefit as the other. Through kindness, love, gifts, invites, the value of relationships benefit each one equally. One may be better at coordinating outings and the other may be more demonstrative with gifts. But the balance and the value between the two is levelled off in that sweet spot found in the middle.

SELF-GUIDED WORKSHEET

1. Note the top 5 relationships in your life.

_____

_____

_____

_____

_____

_____

_____

_____

_____

_____

2. For each one you noted, write down how balanced they
   are with the principles noted: (Scale of 1-5 with 5 being
   completely balanced).

_____

_____

_____

_____

_____

_____

_____

_____

_____

3. For those that didn't receive stellar 5's, what can be done
   to improve them?

_____

_____

_____

_____

_____

_____

_____

_____

_____

_____

4. Are there some relationships that are no longer serving
   you?

_____

_____

_____

_____

_____

_____

_____

_____

_____

_____

5. What are some relationships you feel you could work to make better?

_____

_____

_____

_____

_____

_____

_____

_____

_____

_____

_____

6. Create action plans to repair or remove those that aren't healthy for you anymore.

_____

_____

_____

_____

_____

_____

_____

_____

_____

_____

_____

7. What the relationships in your life that you feel you can spend more time nurturing?

_____

_____

_____

_____

_____

_____

_____

_____

_____

_____

8. How will you feel when you make some edits in your relationships?

_____

_____

_____

_____

_____

_____

_____

_____

_____

THE GURU SYNOPSIS

Humans should strive to have balanced relationships. At times, in relationships, the balance can get thrown off due to life changes and natural shifts. The key is to have the relationship hover in the space that flows in a seesaw formation and it averages out to a 50/50 split of energy given and received. It's important to have healthy relationships so our emotional and supportive network is there to assist us through life.

PERSONAL MANTRA TEMPLATE

I will seek to nurture relationships that are healthy.
I will remove the relationships that do not serve my soul.
I will respect my soul by creating fulfilling relationships.
I will be intentional in creating balance in my relationships.

Lesson 10:
faith

We were pregnant with our third and final little human. We splurged to have the very fancy and pricey 4-D ultrasound. The images showed something unusual and confirmed that there were a few issues concerning the pregnancy. We were dealing with a single uterine artery and a hole in my amniotic sac combined withmy body's historical and natural act of going into preterm labor. I left the doctor's office in tears after hearing their warnings and preparing myself for what to expect in the worst case scenario. Spiritually, I was doomed, and I started to grieve what was ahead for us. I unintentionally dedicated a day to sadness while crying on our sofa. I thought about faith, what it meant to have authentic faith and the purpose of it in our lives.

After a few hours of meditation and reflection, a sense of peace set in and my tears were replaced with a sense of Godly calmness. All the fears, doubt, and horrible stories playing in my mind seemed to be replaced with a non-human sense of grace and blessings. At that moment, I absorbed and embraced the true belief in the word, faith.

Humans of faith understand there is divinity in each path we take in life. Those who have faith grieve but find a light at that moment to connect to something greater than themselves, and love themselves and others more deeply. When we surrender to life situations in which we have no control, faith is there to lead our hearts into healing. Combined with faith comes the power of positive thinking. Some humans use the power of positive thinking, envisionment in prayer, or meditation to move the heart into a place of surrender and grace.

My grandmother suffered from cancer and during her last week of life, I was at her side with her rosary. The intense reality of her condition gripped me and sent my heart into the deepest grief I had yet felt. She was a remarkable woman with various PhDs and a daily yoga routine. She was one of those iconic women who was cast in her own mold. While at her side during her last few breaths, a moment of faith and surrender flourished within me. I felt light and comforted in knowing that even with the heartbreak, her transition and my healing would be guided. Faith gave me peace in knowing she would still be connected to me not physically, but spiritually with her transition and passing. I realized, if I truly had faith and the belief in the after, then the surrender is inevitable and part of the process.

While in Bali a few years ago, I asked our guide why some trees were wrapped in black and white checkered cloth. He shared that the wrap is called a saput poleng cloth and it is a symbolism of the Balinese philosophy of balance called Rwa Bhineda. The Balinese believe there is no joy without sorrow, no night without day. They understand that there will always be good and bad in the world and in every human. Their goal is to make efforts for balance and happiness for all of us. When we accept and embrace the ups and downs of life, the 'faith and surrender' narrative becomes a more natural process of living.

SELF-GUIDED WORKSHEET

Our lives are filled with moments of surrendering to Spirit and letting go of the stresses that consume us.

1. What are the current situations in your life that you have no control over?

_____

_____

_____

_____

_____

_____

_____

_____

_____

_____

2. What are the negative thoughts that circle through your mind when you think of this situation? Note up to 5 only.

_____

_____

_____

_____

_____

_____

3. Write out the ways it's better for you to release and
   surrender this situation and how it will benefit you.

---

4. What is one area of your life where you feel you need
   more grace in? Write it here with detail.

---

5. Let's change the perspective in this area. If you could see this scenario from the perspective of your best friend, what would be the blessings and lessons you would gain? Often in the dark, we find our own undiscovered beauty. What would be your own beauty here?

_____

_____

_____

_____

_____

_____

_____

_____

_____

_____

6. When was the last time you felt connected to the concept of surrendering and faith?

_____

_____

_____

_____

_____

_____

_____

7. What are some personal ways you can increase your faith?

_____

_____

_____

_____

_____

_____

_____

_____

_____

_____

8. What are some actions that you can take on to work on your spiritual growth?

_____

_____

_____

_____

_____

_____

_____

_____

_____

_____

9. Write down 3-5 humans who you know can help you develop the faith component of your life?

_____

_____

_____

_____

_____

_____

_____

_____

_____

_____

10. How will you honor yourself more with your deep development of faith? development of faith?

_____

_____

_____

_____

_____

_____

_____

_____

_____

_____

_____

Faith allows us to remove a burden and replace it with the knowledge that our lesson is in its surrender.

THE GURU SYNOPSIS

My intention in sharing these stories and self-guided work is to illustrate the value and comfort in surrendering. Sometimes the best decision is to just let go and allow things to find their place no matter the darkness or pain. Surrendering can be one of the most powerful acts in the alignment of your shift. There is beauty within you and faith grows in accordance to the love for yourself, your path and your spirit.

PERSONAL MANTRA TEMPLATE

I will surrender to scenarios I have no control of.
I recognize there is beauty in holding faith in my life.
I will work to increase faith that fits
my higher purpose and connectivity .
I will intentionally dedicate time in my daily life
to serving my spirituality through
meditation, prayer and peaceful reflection.

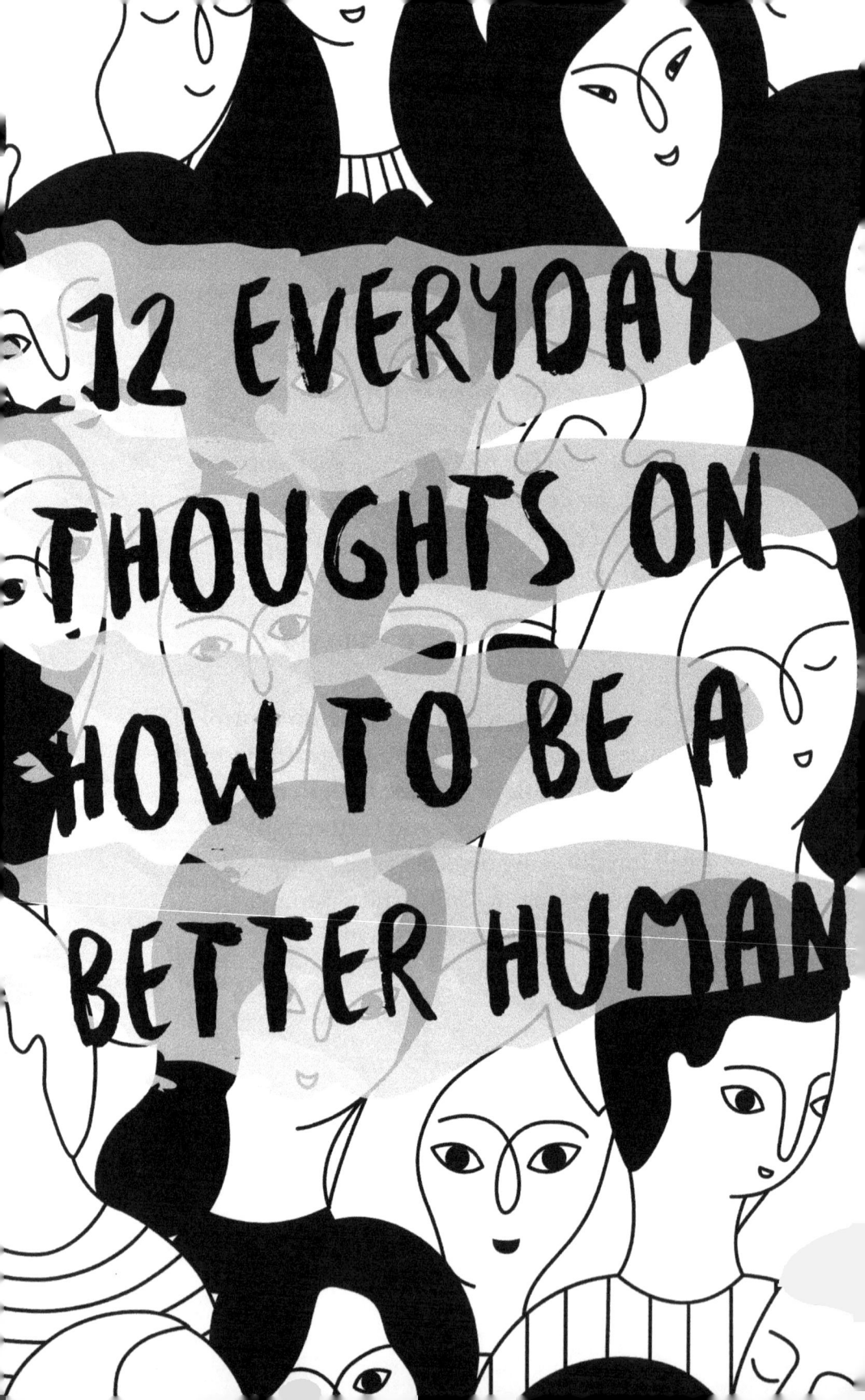

12 EVERYDAY THOUGHTS ON HOW TO BE A BETTER HUMAN

I n closing, I would like to share 12 everyday thoughts on how to be a better human.

1. Speak words that come from love and ask prior to speaking, does this elevate the conversation to a higher level?

2. Remove the defining physical or religious characteristics of each person you chat with and look only at their soul level.

3. Everyone has been through a lot. I am the story of someone who was abused, who had a mom suffering from addiction, my childhood had moments of violence, I went from welfare to wealth. We all have stories. You have a choice to step forward with forgiveness or sit and hold yourself back in anger for what you have been through. Once you make the choice to move forward and leave the past behind, life and opportunities will get better and easier.

4. People can sense your energy from far away. Regardless of the words that you use, they can intuitively feel your spirit. If you find yourself in a bad funk and not feeling your happy groove, repeat this mantra "I am in harmony with God, I am in harmony with life, I am in harmony with love and I am in harmony with peace". Repeat until you elevate your spirit and the foggy cloud moves away. You can replace God with Jesus, Universe, higher being...

5. Be the voice for others who can't share their own.

6. Be of service to the world and each day ask yourself, "How can my presence help others?"

7. Spend a few moments a day acknowledging your beauty, strengths, value and worth. Pat yourself on the back and share kind words.

8. When you are blessed, take a moment and provide the opportunity of being blessed to another person.

9. One act of kindness can be shared through text, phone calls, in-person and it's free. Schedule a time block to share gratitude with others.

10. Surround yourself with those who bring you utmost joy in a healthy way.

11. Dedicate moments of your week to be in solitude, peace and around nature. This is where you will strengthen your connection, purpose and clarity.

12. Be your biggest cheerleader and believe that your power, presence and existence is a gift that is connected to a higher purpose.

13. I am celebrating your soulful evolution and spiritual connection to your self-guided guru.

With love, peace and gratitude,

Violette de Ayala

ABOUT THE AUTHOR

Violette de Ayala is Cuban American, the mother of 3 humans and 1 non-human. She is the Founder of FemCity serving as a catalyst for community creations and helping women foster relationships through personal and business development. Each FemCity community gathers monthly and leads with a mantra of gratitude for the self and for other women around the world. FemCity is on a mission to serve over 1 million women around the world and inspire women to collaborate, design and build their lives and businesses through community and gratitude.

CONNECT WITH VIOLETTE

Violette would love to hear from you. She invites you to email her at hello@violettedeayala.com. You can also follow her on Instagram and Twitter @violettedeayala.

Violette is also available to inspire and motivate your team, organization, or audience. She tours often, coaches in the wealth and mindset themes, speaks passionately and is focused on engaging humans to move forward in purpose and love. If you're interested in having Violette come to your event, please visit violettedeayala.com/speaking.

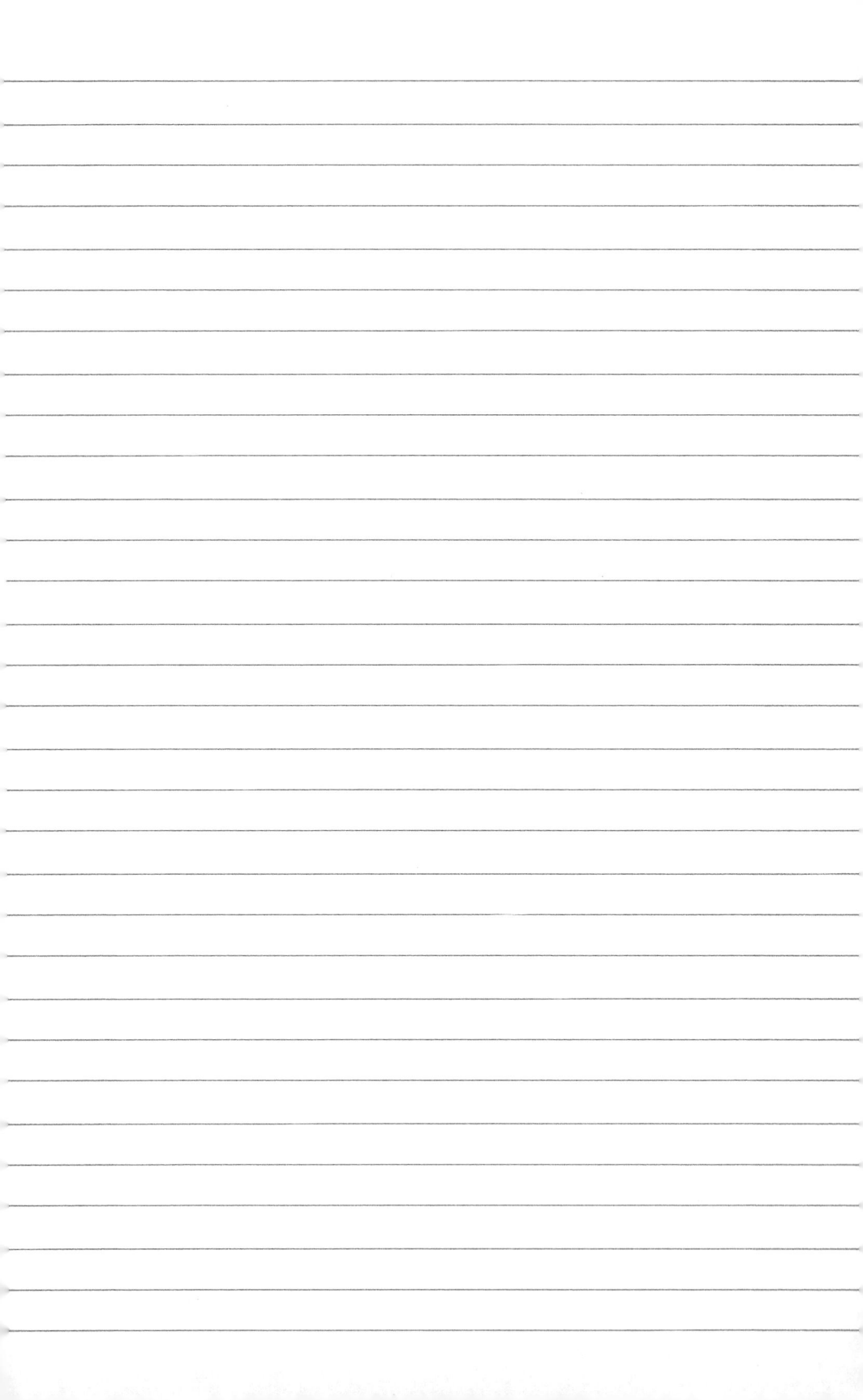

www.ingramcontent.com/pod-product-compliance
Lightning Source LLC
LaVergne TN
LVHW041230080426
835508LV00011B/1146